Victorian Parlors

and

Tea Parties

Patricia B. Mitchell

*Published 1991 by the author at the
Sims-Mitchell House Bed & Breakfast,
P. O. Box 429, Chatham, VA 24531.
    Tel/fax: 804-432-0595
    E-mail: answers@foodhistory.com
    Website: www.foodhistory.com*

*Printed in the U. S. A.
ISBN 0-925117-36-6*

Ninth Printing, May 2000

- Illustrations -

*Front Cover - a collage of "Gibson Girl" illustrations
    by Charles Dana Gibson, provided by Dover
    Publications, Inc., New York.*

*Inside Title Page and Back Cover - provided by Dover
    Publications, Inc.*

*Inside Back Cover - portrait of the author by David L.
    Mitchell.*

Table of Contents

Chapter 1

The Tea Meal and How It Came to Be

Tradition has it that the ritual of afternoon tea was begun in England by Anna, the seventh duchess of Bedford (1783-1857). At that time dinner was served quite late, during lengthy summer days, so there was a long interval between breakfast and the evening meal. The duchess experienced a "sinking feeling" in the afternoons, so she ordered her servants to send up snacks of small cakes, [1] biscuits, tarts, cheesecake, "mackeroons," and bread spread with "good sweet butter." The *petit* repast was accompanied by tea. [2]

No doubt this dose of carbohydrates briefly corrected her low blood sugar, and the caffeine zing from "the cup that cheers but not inebriates" gave her a lift. Soon Anna's court friends copied her, and serving late afternoon tea and refreshments became the *chic* thing to do.

The fashionable tea meal was adopted in the United States, where affluent ladies emulated the English socialites. Low tables were set near sofas and chairs, and laid with the finest linen, china, and silver. This pretty show of elegance enjoyed a spate of popularity, but then tea and Anglomania went out of vogue as the Parliament levied new taxes and colonists responded with a boycott of English tea that culminated in the "Boston Tea Party" of 1773. Tea consumption dropped dramatically, and it was not until April 27, 1776, that Congress advertised in the Philadelphia *Packet* that ". . . the drinking of tea can now be indulged." [3] Americans began to again enjoy the beverage and the tea party slowly regained ascendance. A century later, in the mid-1800's, an appreciation of the nation's English heritage was rekindled. The approaching centennial, and admiration of Queen Victoria's successful rule of Brittania, sparked people's enthusiasm for British ways. The styles and habits of England were suddenly dear to U. S. citizens. One of the results of this obsession with English life was the revival of "kettledrums" or afternoon tea. This mini-meal was an opportunity for ladies to boil up some water in the teakettle and have a social event.

In Oscar Wilde's *The Importance of Being Earnest* Algernon says, "I believe it is customary in good society to take some slight refreshment at five o'clock . . ." Jack asks (in a few minutes): "Why all these cups? Why cucumber sandwiches? Why such reckless extravagance in one so young? Who is coming to tea?" [4]

Elaborate teas were never, of course, part of the social life of the working-class. Only those with money and refined social skills carried out this urbane form of entertaining. Middle-class women had friends over for visits, but usually those without servants were so busy operating the household and tending to children that there was little leisure time for formal parties. About such "ordinary" people in a New England suburb it was reported:

> *"Of almost every one of these little households it may be said that a woman is the main-spring; the men are away all day, and it is the wife or mother who gives tone and character to the house.*
>
> *"These women vary greatly in education, refinement, enlightenment, but certain qualities they have all in common; they are with scarcely an exception, energetic, practical, and 'smart' ... these executive qualities are rarely wanting. You see it in the look of their houses and dinner tables, in their children's dress and their own, and in the standing of the children at school."* [5]

That passage gives insight into the importance of hearth and home to the Victorians. To them home was the center of the universe, and as much as possible, time and energy were invested on the home front. In 1884 an issue of *Our Homes and Their Adornments* proclaimed, "Home is 'embalmed in song, cherished in the memory, and enshrined in the heart.'" [6]

". . . Home became a banner, something to be held aloft and pressed forward. It showed where a man had got to, and he clung to it and waved it until the day came when he could exchange it for a bigger and better one." [7]

Chapter II

The Role of the Victorian Wife
and
Her Political and Economic Emergence

Some women found it necessary to work in factories, teach, or become nurses or domestics, but most chose to marry. The prospect of the companionship of a husband and children held tremendous appeal. A few women, like Florence Nightingale longed for "a profession, a trade, a necessary occupation, something to fill and employ all my faculties," [8] but a majority were content to be homemakers. Among those blessed with material possessions, there was quite a home "to make."

The "socially approved sloth" [9] of the prosperous Victorian lady was an illusion, for she "often had to toil desperately behind the scenes in order to seem to be doing nothing in front of them." [10] Not only did she have to manage and instruct her servants and children, she had to "beautify" her husband's household, in which she was the "chief ornament." [11] To achieve the proper, pure, pallid Victorian look the lady wore a corset, reducing her waist measurement as much as fifteen inches. [12] (In theory a gentleman could imagine encompassing the waist of his beloved within the circle of his hands.) The constriction of steel ribs and whalebone actually interfered with the woman's breathing, making "fainting couches" a useful piece of furniture. The skirt and petticoats of the fashionable Victorian lady might easily weigh fifteen pounds. [13] Such heavy trailing skirts, tight waists, and billowing sleeves taught the well-attired 19th-century woman the "poetry of dependence." [14] This restrictive clothing also made any outdoor work or exercise virtually impossible, thus rendering her a "fragile and delicate houseplant," destined to stay inside most of the time. As Alice L. Powers has observed, ". . . Women at home were supposed to provide a decorative haven for their husbands. Carefully corseted and swaddled in colorful material, they were part of the home decoration."[15]

A lady could easily spend three to four hours a day in the dreary business of dressing and undressing: dress upon arising, change for a morning outing, dress differently for lunch, dress again for tea, and once more for dinner.[16]

The superficially indolent life of the 19th-century wealthy woman emulated the lifestyle of English gentry and other members of European aristocracy.[17] The American Victorians were attempting to develop socio-economic stratification of society, and their barometer was property. Within this system of self-aggrandizement, dressing and entertaining in a lavish, even ostentatious manner served its purpose — separating the rich, genteel leisure class from "have-nots." The affluent man desired that his wife be "useless,"[18] since human function and utility bespoke "working-class."

A prosperous, respectable Victorian husband would in truth have been humiliated if he had been unable to support in style his dependents, including wife, children, servants, and single or widowed female relatives. The man prided himself on keeping his wife at home where the duties of household supervision, child care, and personal *toilette* took up her time. Despite such responsibilities, the Victorian wife was also expected to be "clever with her fingers,"[19] producing numerous home crafts — never to sell for profit — like beadwork, shellwork, and needlework. Moreover, the isolation of being a stay-at-home created a woman wont to entertain. Luncheons, dinners, and tea parties became the Victorian ladies' *forté*, and her window to the world. Reciprocal visits to the houses of her friends were socially acceptable excursions.

In this seemingly self-indulgent, boring sphere of leisure and dependence upon men the Victorian female discovered a secret pay-off: being a "kept woman" allowed her time for intellectual and spiritual advancement, and an eventual desire for social reform.[20] In fact, it has been said that "moral reform was the luxury of the lady of leisure; economic progress was the necessity of the woman who had to earn her bread."[21]

Despite 18th-century novelist Henry Fielding's comment that "Love and scandal are the best sweeteners of tea,"[22] and 19th-century writer Oliver Wendell Holmes's rather unflattering, yet funny, description of a tea party as ". . . giggle, gabble, gobble, and git . . .,"[23] women did actually reach beyond the facade of superficiality of chit-chat and converse on deeper topics, and at tea tables perhaps were whispered comments such as "Would it not be advantageous for Daughter to attend a college?" or "If women could vote . . ." or "I think that someone would actually *pay* me to make a christening gown for her baby."

At the tea parties in houses near Seneca Falls, New York, Elizabeth Stanton met with Lucretia Mott and her circle of Quaker women in 1848. These two reformers planned a convention on women's rights, the first such political gathering.[24] American women had learned to organize themselves for social outreach and charitable causes under the auspices of the Protestant evangelical churches. Thanks to the Victorians' commitment to the importance of individual responsibility, women involved themselves in missionary and Bible societies and other church organizations championing worthy causes. Thus, ladies learned to raise funds and finance speakers, and to work as a team.[25] As Sallie Cotton, a North Carolinian who helped to organize women's groups, expressed it, "the new force in modern civilization . . . is educated, Christianized, organized womanhood."[26]

Compassionate women sensed the plight of the less fortunate, and were motivated to change the world. Often the staging area for this battle was the parlor where friends met for culinary refreshments and spiritual and mental inspiration. The discussion of high ideals (as well as trivial details — Jane Austen, in writing to her sister Cassandra, speaks about materials she had bought for gowns and "whim-whams and fribble-frabble of fashion")[27] took place in the room reserved for guests, the Victorian parlor. It could be stated that if the kitchen is (and was) the heart of the house; then the parlor was the larynx, for that room bespoke of the family's status, personal tastes, places visited, as well as serving as a *"salon."*

Chapter III

Victorian Parlors and Exteriors:
Inner Space and Outer Grace

Numerous people today have an erroneous impression that the interiors of Victorian homes were depressingly dark and chaotically cluttered. These ideas are only partial truths - the well-decorated 19th-century house usually had darkly stained woodwork and furniture and deep, rich patterns of wallpaper. The walls were art-gallery-esque, and all available surfaces were display areas for "various kinds of fancy work and small decorative trifles." [28]

Nevertheless this combination of factors did not produce the somber hodge-podge one might expect. The authentic Victorian wallpaper we see now has faded and become dirty, its magical "bloom" being obscured. The Victorians used gold, silver, and bronze flecks in the wallpapers to achieve a radiant luster. Flocks and embossing also lent sheen and excitement to the wallcoverings. [29] Moreover, the Victorians frequently used more than one pattern of paper in the same room, adding to the explosion of optical stimuli. Woodwork was kept nicely polished, creating more rich glow. Stained-glass windows and regular windows as well as lamplight added subtle shimmer.

The array of objects and trinkets was not disconcerting because things were kept in order. — Comfort, snugness, and coziness were words especially associated with the reign of Queen Victoria, and comfort was considered inseparable from tidiness. [30]

Maintaining the collection of bric-a-brac so typical of the spacious Victorian house was a tedious, never-ending task. Dusting and arranging the charming *potpourri* of possessions could occupy the time and concentration of a museum curator. The well-regulated Victorian home was organized with everything in its place. The lavishness and abundance of decor imparted a feeling of security, not pandemonium.

The exterior of the Victorian mansion, whether it was Queen Anne (dubbed a "tossed salad of Elizabethan, Jacobean, Oriental, Indian, and classical" architecture[31]); French Mansard (or Second Empire); Gothic; Italianate; or early Stick, was never visually boring. Andrew Jackson Downing, an architect of the period, wrote in 1842, "There is one colour . . . frequently employed by house painters, which we feel bound to protest *against* most heartily, as entirely unsuitable, and in bad taste. This is *white*, which is so universally applied to our wooden houses of every size and description . . . (and) unpleasant to an eye attuned to harmony of coloring." [32] The colors prescribed by Downing were natural earth tones. Other house designers suggested even more vivid shades, and since the paint used was linseed-oil based, the exteriors possessed a "bloom," a luminescence, similar to that within the chandelier-lit parlors. As many as five different colors were used on the outside of the house.

The exterior of the abode, often encrusted with "gingerbread" (the millwork cornucopia of decorative brackets, graceful latticework and spindles, etc.) vied with the interior in attention to detail. Simple draperies were not enough; one window could easily accomodate opulent draperies and ornate valances, muslin curtains, blinds, and wooden shutters. Because the Romantic Movement venerated nature, the Victorians were the first to construct bay windows, all the better to see the beauty of the out-of-doors (beyond the layers of window treatments). They built gazebos and designed informal gardens, and brought this passion for nature inside in the form of shell art, feather-work, collections of natural objects and in motifs from nature. Flower designs were popular, and the floral theme adorned fabrics, wallpaper, china tiles, and cast iron. Preserved butterflies and taxidermied animals and birds demonstrated the Victorian interest in zoology and natural history. Scrimshaw was appreciated.

In addition to all this, the Victorian parlor could sport ceiling fans, moulding, medallions, borders, stenciling, friezes, fireplaces, parquetry floors, and perhaps even a Turkish-style tented section of the room. Because the parlor was normally reserved for guests, very little rearranging of furniture was necessary when the lady chose to entertain. Perhaps a few chairs were moved to prepare for a tea party.

> *"There were lots of chairs in Victorian rooms because a gentleman would always stand up when a lady entered the room; yet as he wouldn't think of allowing her to sit in his warmed chair, there always had to be a cool one at the ready."* [33]

A side table was set with the best of china and accoutrements, all artistically laid out. Light from oil lamps, and either a gas or electric fixture diffused the room, causing the tea service to glisten. A last minute dusting of the glass domes under which rested various treasures, a moment spent lighting a *pastille* or fragrance cone, and the Victorian homemaker was ready to greet her guests. "Time for tea!"

Chapter IV

In Order That the Stomach
Not Remain Inactive . . .

Arnold Palmer, in his book *Movable Feasts*, reveals that ". . . the stomach, the English stomach, does not care to remain inactive for more than four or five hours . . . " [34] The following recipes and remarks will satisfy English and kindred digestive systems, and stimulate the intellect.

"Tea and crumpets" is an oft-heard Anglophile's expression. Crumpets are small round breads baked in metal rings on a griddle. (Crumpets are baked on one side until the batter has bubbles "baked in" and then they are baked only briefly on the other side. "English" muffins are baked evenly on both sides.[35]) Pikelets are similar, but their batter is baked without the use of metal rings on a griddle, bakestone, or in a skillet. These breads are akin to a thick pancake, and are not sweet. They are usually served toasted and buttered, perhaps with jam.[36]

Scones taste like rich baking powder biscuits. Originally they were baked on a cast iron griddle or in a skillet over an open fire. They were made in medieval England and Wales, although the name is derived from "*schönbrot*," meaning "fine bread" or "beautiful bread" in German. They were first made with oats or barley flour formed into rounds, then cut into wedges and cooked.[37] Other students of etymology have pointed out that the word "scone" (it rhymes with "gone") is related to the Gaelic word "*sgonn*" [38] and the Dutch word *schoonbrot*" [39]. "*Sgonn*" translates "large mouthful." [40] In any tongue, though, scones make happy palates.

The scones we have encountered in our travels in England and the British-cultured Bahamas happened to have been either plain scones made with white flour or plain ones with currants. The following derivations are more healthful because whole wheat flour is used and very little fat. For fun, scone dough can be cut into heart, diamond, or other shapes. Just add a little additional flour to make the dough slightly stiffer, and cut out shapes with cookie cutters.

Honey-Prune-Walnut Scones

4 c. whole wheat flour
1 tbsp. baking powder
1/2 tsp. salt
1/2 tsp. soda
1/4 c. vegetable oil
1/4 c. honey

1 c. pitted prunes, chopped (or 1 c. dates, chopped)
1 c. walnuts, chopped
1 2/3 c. sour milk* or buttermilk

Mix together the first four ingredients. In a large bowl mix the remaining ingredients. Stir in the dry mixture, mixing well. Using your hands, form two balls of dough. Flatten these balls on a floured surface to 3/4 inch thick. Cut each disc into wedges. (Small wedges are more ladylike for tea parties — we like 'em big at breakfast.) Place the wedges on baking sheets and bake at 375° F. for approximately 10 minutes or until the bottoms have browned slightly. Turn over the wedges and bake about 5 minutes more.

*Note: For sour milk, put 2 scant tablespoons vinegar or lemon juice in a pint measuring cup. Add milk (I use reconstituted nonfat powdered milk) to equal 1 2/3 c. liquid. Let sit a few minutes for it to "sour."

Lady Astor Apple Scones

These "let's-celebrate-something" Lady Astor Apple Scones are named in honor of Lady Astor (1879-1964), the first woman member of the British House of Commons. The Viscountess was born Nancy Langhorne in Danville, Virginia, a town 18 miles south of Chatham, the home of your authoress. (Incidentally, Nancy's look-alike older sister Irene was a model for her husband Charles Dana Gibson's famous "Gibson Girl" images, such as are seen on the front cover of this book.) Those American girls who "made good" would probably enjoy these delectable scones, a merger of English breadstuff and "good ole new" American ideas of nutrition: whole wheat flour and fresh fruit.

* * *

4 c. whole wheat flour
1 tbsp. baking powder
1/2 tsp. salt
1 tbsp. cinnamon
1/2 tsp. cloves

1 lg. unpeeled apple, chopped
3 tbsp. vegetable oil
1/4 c. honey
1 1/2 c. milk

Mix the dry ingredients. In another bowl mix the remaining things. Stir together the two mixtures. Knead the dough slightly and form two balls. Flatten these balls to a thickness of about 3/4 of an inch, and cut into wedges. (Round shapes can also be cut — just roll out the entire amount of dough to a thickness of 1/2 - 3/4 inch and cut out.) When the scones are cut place them on baking sheets. Bake in a pre-heated 400° F. oven for approximately 12 minutes. If the bottoms brown too rapidly, turn them over.

Follow the preceding instructions for preparing scones to create the next two flavorful breads.

High Society Spicy Currant Scones

4 c. whole wheat flour
2 tsp. baking powder
1/2 tsp. salt
1 tsp. baking soda
2 tsp. cinnamon
1/2 tsp. nutmeg
1 tbsp. grated orange peel
1/4 c. honey
1/2 c. currants (or raisins)
Approximately 1 2/3 c. milk

Proceed as in other scone recipes.

Sesame-Orange Scones

The Mitchell family likes scones. Having tested lots of scone recipes, we figured that this one, since it doesn't have "fancy" ingredients like dates, walnuts, or such, would probably be rather ho-hum. We were pleased to find that *these Sesame-Orange Scones are really extra-nice. The Victorians who first lived in our house would have found them to be quite commendable.*

* * *

4 c. whole wheat flour
2 tsp. baking powder
1/2 tsp. salt
1 tsp. grated orange peel
2 tbsp. vegetable oil
1/4 c. honey or sugar
1 c. orange juice
1/3 c. water (approximately)

Topping:

1 tbsp. butter or margarine
2 tbsp. sesame seeds

Prepare the scones in the manner described in the other scone recipes, up to the point of having formed 2 balls and flattened them. At this time, melt the butter and stir in the sesame seeds. Pat this butter/seed mixture over the tops of the disks; cut into wedges; and bake at 400° F. for around 12 minutes, or until the bottoms are pale brown.

Other treats for the Victorian tea table might include the following goodies.

Albert & Victoria Crackers

1 1/2 c. whole wheat flour
1/2 tsp. caraway seeds
1/2 tsp. onion powder
1/2 c. Cheddar cheese, grated
2 tbsp. oil
Water to moisten

Mix the dry ingredients. Add oil and enough water to make a damp batter. Form a ball and then roll out thinly on a floured surface. Cut into squares or other shapes and bake at 350° F. until barely browned.

These crackers taste best if served warmed. They are fine eaten plain or as vehicles for such spreads as the English person's dearly loved potted meats.

High Muck-a-Muck Crabmeat Spread

1 lb. cooked crabmeat, chopped
1 c. Cheddar cheese, grated
1/3 c. mayonnaise
2 green onions, finely chopped

Mix. Spread on toast rounds, triangles, or crackers. Heat 5-10 minutes at 400° F. (until hot and bubbly). Serve hot.

Teatime reached the "pinnacle of plenitude" [41] with the Victorian high tea, which was really a meal. The menu usually included a pair of savory dishes, cold roasted fowl and meat, salads, cakes, tarts and custards. Several different blends of tea and a selection of liquors were poured. [42]

Silk Stocking Seafood Salad

1 c. cooked crabmeat or lobster or shrimp, chopped
1 c. celery, chopped
1 tbsp. pimiento, chopped
1 tbsp. lemon juice
Salt and pepper
Mayonnaise to moisten

Combine everything and chill.

Chicken Salad Elegant

2 c. cooked chicken, chopped
1/2 - 1 tsp. curry powder (optional)

1/4 c. almonds, chopped
Salt to taste
1 1/2 c. seedless grapes, peeled (Tokay grapes are best)
1 1/2 c. celery, chopped
1/2 c. mayonnaise
1/4 c. sour cream

Combine all ingredients. Divide into four portions and serve on lettuce or in cheese pastry shells:

1 c. sifted flour
1 tsp. salt
1/2 c. Cheddar cheese, finely grated
1/3 c. shortening
2 1/2 - 3 tbsp. very cold water

Mix flour, salt, and cheese with a fork. Blend in shortening. Add water slowly, stirring all the while, until the mixture will form a ball. Pinch off small balls of dough. With a rolling pin, roll out the small balls of pastry between two sheets of wax paper. Roll them until they are about 1/8-inch thick. Turn a muffin tin upside down and shape the circles of pastry around the muffin cups. Bake the pastry, still on the inverted muffin tin, at 350° F. about 20 minutes or until slightly brown. When the shells cool, they will be crisp. Store in tins. Delicious and special filled with Chicken Salad Elegant (or turkey or tuna salad).[43]

Potwalloper* Fish Sandwiches

Mashed sardines or tuna
Mashed hard-cooked eggs
Butter, softened
Parsley, chopped
Black pepper
Cayenne
Mustard
Paprika

Use thin slices of bread with the crusts removed. Butter the bread. Combine the above ingredients and spread on bread. Cut into oblong shapes.

*Note: A "potwalloper" is an English householder.

Savory Sandwiches

3 tbsp. butter
1 tsp. capers
6 olives
1 tbsp. chopped mustard pickle
2 tsp. chopped parsley
A few drops of onion juice
Slices of buttered white or Graham bread

"Beat the butter to a cream, add the capers and olives chopped finely; mix these well with the butter and stir in the pickle, parsley and onion juice, with salt if necessary. Spread between slices of either white or Graham bread, well buttered." [44]

High-Toned Cucumber Sandwiches

2 cucumbers
1 tsp. onion juice
1/3 c. mayonnaise
Salt and pepper
Slices of buttered bread

"Peel the cucumbers and remove the seeds if coarse; chop the cucumbers finely and place them in a cloth or a sieve to drain. To the drained pulp add the onion juice, seasoning and mayonnaise. Spread between slices of buttered whole wheat or Graham bread." [45]

Oyster Patty Filling

1/3 c. butter
1/2 c. flour
3 c. milk
1 tsp. salt
1/4 tsp. paprika
1 pint small oysters
6 small pastry shells

"Melt butter and add flour. Blend well and add milk, salt, and paprika. Cook slowly and stir constanty until very thick sauce forms. Add oysters which have been carefully looked over and heated. Serve at once in hot pastry shells." [46]

In some cases Americans speak a different English from that spoken in Great Britain. For instance, in England what we call cookies are referred to as biscuits. (Technically speaking, "biscuit" is a French term applied to a floury confection which undergoes double baking.) The following recipe is for non-sweet American biscuits. For tea meals make itsy-bitsy biscuits.

Well-Bred Cheddar Cheese Biscuits

1/2 c. sharp Cheddar, grated
1/2 c. soft butter
Dash of cayenne pepper
1 tsp. chutney
1 c. flour

Mix the first 4 ingredients until light and fluffy. Slowly stir in flour, forming a smooth dough. Wrap in plastic wrap and chill 1 hour. Shape into little biscuits; place on an ungreased baking sheet. Bake at 400° F. for approximately 10 minutes or until just brown.

Inhabitants of Great Britain seem to have insatiable sweet tooths. Jam, jellies, conserves, preserves, and the like are an integral part of tea time. Clotted cream, another tea time food, might require an explanation. Think "whipped cream." This thick dairy product is used as a bread spread like butter, though some people use jam, clotted cream, *and butter* simultaneously on their scones, sponge cake, etc.

Fig Preserves with Black Walnuts

"Pare figs, cover well with sugar and let sit overnight. Turn into preserving kettle and let cook two hours. To one

cup of fruit, add one cup of sugar and juice of a large lemon. Let cook until transparent and until it will 'jelly' which will be two hours or more. Stir frequently to prevent burning. Half an hour before removing from fire, add slightly chopped walnuts (about 1/2 cup to a pint of fruit). Put in small jars or jelly tumblers." [47]

English Orange Marmalade

4 Oranges
1/2 Grapefruit
1/3 Lemon
Sugar

   "Remove seeds from fruit. Cut fruit into very thin slices. Cut each slice in quarters. Remove pithy inner portion from each section of fruit. Add 1 1/2 quarts water to each pound of fruit. Let stand 24 hours. Boil hard 1 hour. Add 1 pound sugar to each pound fruit and liquid. Boil slowly 45 minutes or until juice sheets from spoon." [48]

   Victorians found tea refreshments to be useful for various entertainments — high tea (more a light supper), family tea, nursery tea, bridge teas, tennis teas, wedding teas, and tea dances. [49]

Tea Dance Date-Nut Bread

1 1/2 c. white flour
5 tsp. baking powder
1 1/2 tsp. salt
1/4 tsp. soda
1 1/2 c. whole wheat flour
1 c. dates, chopped
1 c. nuts, chopped
1/2 c. brown sugar
1 1/2 c. milk
1/4 c. molasses

   Combine the dry ingredients. Stir in milk and molasses, and spoon into a greased loaf pan. Bake at 375° F. for about an hour. To serve at tea time, slice and then cut each slice in half (or bake two mini-loaves, reducing oven time). Delicious spread with cream cheese.

Vanderbilt Bread

This richly spiced bread is a favorite at our house for "nursery tea," i. e., the children's snack time.

* * *

3 3/4 c. whole wheat flour
1 1/2 tsp. baking powder
1 1/2 tsp. baking soda
1/4 tsp. salt
1 tbsp. cinnamon
1 tsp. nutmeg
1/2 tsp. allspice
1/2 c. brown sugar, firmly packed
2 1/3 c. sour milk or buttermilk

Mix together everything except the sour milk. Stir in the sour milk, moistening completely. Spoon the batter into two greased 8x4-inch loaf pans, and bake in a preheated 350° F. oven for about 40 minutes (or until a toothpick inserted near the center comes out clean). Makes 2 smallish loaves. [Note: For a bigger, "family-sized" loaf, spoon the batter into a greased 9x5-inch loaf pan and bake close to an hour, or until the loaf tests done.]

The Victorian Age was an era of startling advancement in technology and science, the zenith of the Industrial Revolution. Yet, as a counterpoint to the emphasis on function, utility, and efficiency, the Victorians reveled in form and superfluity in the applied arts. Houses were statements of whimsy and froufrou, clothing fashions a pronouncement of elegance and impracticality, and food ofttimes an artful parody. For example, a popular recipe involved baking pound cake in a four-quart rounded metal bowl, and tinting the raisin-strewn batter red with beet juice.

A buttercream frosting colored with spinach juice topped the cake in order to achieve the appearance of a watermelon.

The playful, showy touches in architecture, cuisine, etc. were themselves by-products of technical progress. Steam and foot treadle-driven jigsaws, scroll saws, and band saws made gingerbread house trim easily feasible. (The term gingerbread comes from the Medieval French word "*gingimbrat*," meaning preserved ginger. This evolved into the cake-like gingerbread of English lore which was originally baked in many fanciful shapes. The word gingerbread was then applied to decorations on sailing ships, and eventually to carved house ornamentations.)[50]

Scientific research and invention also made kitchen work faster and easier, and allowed the creative cook, under the direction of the mistress of the house, increased opportunities to exhibit skills in preparing fancifully prepared and arranged foods. More modern stoves, iceboxes and refrigerators, and other equipment were tools used to create tempting kickshaws (appetizers), itty-bitty tarts, myriads of candies, and other non-essential edibles.

A further strange dichotomy of the Victorian period was a conservatism in speech, the antithesis of the liberally decorated world around these paradoxical people. As Michael Smith points out in his *Afternoon Teabook*, a lady tended to describe as "nice" all things bright and beautiful. Something absolutely fabulous was "*very* nice." Dreadful, ghastly, horrible things were "not very nice." One did not exaggerate or engage in hyperbole. Excess in lifestyle was not reflected in language.

I was raised according to Victorian standards and principles because my mother was brought up by her very proper Victorian grandmother. Mother used the same rules to rear me that Grandmother Susan instilled in her. As I was growing up, one did not comment on the food presented at a meal. (It was considered "common" or animalistic to concentrate on food.) If Mother was served appealing refreshments at a social function she might later remark at home that the food was "nice," meaning (I think) "pretty, dainty, expensive, and complicated to prepare." (Imagine how hard it was for her to become reconciled to a daughter with tremendous enthusiasm for big servings of "real" foods — whole grain flours, yogurt, brown rice, sprouts, beans, etc.!) . . . .

The pound cake recipe listed next does not turn out looking like the previously mentioned watermelon . . . .

Sour Cream Pound Cake

2 sticks butter or margarine
3 c. sugar
3 c. flour
1 c. sour cream
1/4 tsp. soda
Pinch salt
6 egg yolks
6 egg whites
1 tsp. vanilla
1/2 tsp. lemon extract
1/2 tsp. mace (or may use all of one kind of flavoring)

"*Cream butter and sugar thoroughly. Add egg yolks one at a time and beat well. Dissolve soda in sour cream and add alternately with the flour. Mix well after each addition. Add flavoring. Fold in well beaten egg whites. Pre-heat oven to 300° F., and bake in a greased and floured tube cake pan approximately two hours.*" [51]

Much-used recipes of the Victorian *cuisinière* were the seed, sponge, and Dundee cakes. (Dundee Cake is a baked version of Christmas plum pudding with glacé cherries, topped with blanched split almonds and glazed with sugared milk.)

Seed Cake

"*One pound of butter, a pound of sifted powdered sugar, rub to a cream; add the yolks of eight eggs, one at a time, one ounce of carroway [caraway] seed, one nutmeg grated, and a teaspoonful of cinnamon. Stir in one pound and a quarter of sifted flour and the stiff-beaten whites of eggs alternately. Bake slowly. "* [62]

The original title of the next recipe seems inaccurate to us moderns, considering the length of time required just to beat the batter!

Quickly-Made Sponge Cake

"Take four eggs, one cup of pulverized sugar; eggs and sugar beaten together until you can not possibly beat any longer, say half an hour at least; one scant cupful of flour, sifted many times, stirred in gradually and lightly; add a pinch of salt and the grated peel of a lemon or any other flavoring. Never fails. " [63]

The following recipe is a late-20th century rendition of sponge cake.

Sponge Cake Mary Jones

Grated peel of 1 lemon
2 1/2 c. sugar
12 medium egg yolks
1 tsp. lemon juice
10 medium egg whites
Salt
3 1/3 c. sifted all-purpose flour

"Bring all ingredients to room temperature. Grate lemon peel onto sugar. Beat egg yolks lightly. Add sugar, then lemon juice. Beat egg whites and pinch of salt until stiff; fold into yolk mixture. Add flour a little at a time, folding in gently. Pour batter into ungreased 10-inch tube pan. Bake at 325° F. for 1 hour. Remove from oven and stand cake upside down on the neck of a bottle until completely cooled.

"Note: If you like a stronger lemon flavor, add the juice of 1 lemon. " [64]

"Well-Turned-Out" One-Egg Cake

2/3 c. sugar
1/4 c. shortening
1/4 tsp. salt
1 tsp. vanilla
Flavoring [flavoring of your choice, if desired]
1 egg
1 1/2 c. flour
1/2 c. milk
2 tsp. baking powder

"Cream shortening and sugar. Add unbeaten egg. Add flavoring. Beat thoroughly. Sift flour, measure, and sift with salt and baking powder. Add alternately with milk to creamed shortening and sugar. Pour into well-oiled loaf pan. Bake in moderate oven [375° F.] for 35 minutes." [55]

For Tea Cakes:

"Prepare one-egg cake batter, and bake in small muffin tins. . . . Food coloring in a number of the pastel shades may be added to portions of the . . . icing. [56]

Boiled Frosting:

1 c. granulated sugar
1/3 c. hot water
1 egg white
1/6 tsp. cream of tartar
1 tsp. flavoring

"Boil the sugar and water together, without stirring, till they form a thread when a little is lifted from the pan; beat the white of the egg, add the cream of tartar and pour the hot syrup over them, beating while doing so. Add the flavoring, and beat till thick enough to spread." [57]

Cream Tarts

"Make them small, of rich paste. Fill them after baking, with whipped cream, and drop a small spot of jelly in each one. The prettiest and most delicate of tarts." [58]

Peach Cream Tarts

"One cup of butter, one cup of nice drippings and a little salt; cut through just enough flour to thoroughly mix (say about a pound of flour), a cup of ice-water, one whole egg, and the yolks of two eggs mixed with a tablespoonful of brown sugar; add to the flour in which you have previously sifted two teaspoonfuls of baking powder. Handle the dough as little as possible in mixing; bake in round rings in a hot oven [425° to 450° F.] until a light brown. When baked sift pulverized sugar over the top and fill the hollow center with a compote of peaches. Heap whipped cream or ice-cream on top of each one, the latter being preferable." [59]

Old-Fashioned Molasses Cookies

3/4 c. shortening
1 c. brown sugar, packed firmly
1 egg
1/4 c. Grandma molasses
1/2 tsp. cloves
2 1/4 c. flour
2 tsp. soda
1/4 tsp. salt
1 tsp. cinnamon
1 tsp. ginger

"Mix shortening and sugar; beat egg, add to the molasses, then combine with sugar mixture. Sift dry ingredients together and mix well. Chill about 2 hours, or overnight. Grease hands and roll in palm of hand about the size of a marble. Bake on greased cookie sheet 10 to 15 minutes in 350° F. oven. Cookies will crack open like ginger snaps." [60]

"Good-Breeding" Lemon Squares

Crust:

2 c. flour
2 sticks margarine
1/2 c. confectioners' sugar

"Melt margarine and then blend with flour and sugar. Pat into 9x13-inch pan. Bake 20 minutes at 350° F."

Topping:

4 eggs
1/4 - 1/3 c. lemon juice
4 tbsp. flour
2 c. sugar
1/2 tsp. salt
1 tsp. baking powder

"Beat eggs and lemon juice. Sift other ingredients together. Add to eggs and lemon juice. Pour on top of crust while hot. Bake 25 minutes more at 350° F. When cool, sprinkle with confectioners' sugar and cut into squares." [61]

Ginger Wafers

"One cup of butter, one cup of sugar, one cup of molasses, half a cup of cold coffee, with two teaspoonfuls of soda, one tablespoonful of ginger, and flour enough to make a dough stiff enough to roll out thin. Cut with cooky-cutter; bake in quick oven [425° F.]." [62]

Tea Ice Cream

"Steep two ounces of the best mixed tea in three pints of boiling cream. In the meantime stir three-quarters of a pound of pulverized sugar and the yolks of twelve eggs or more until thick; add gradually to the cream, boil up once, strain through a hair sieve, stirring until cold. Freeze." [63]

Ambrosia Ice Cream

1/2 c. shredded candied pineapple
1/4 c. any fruit juice
1/3 c. water
1 c. whipping cream

1/2 c. diced maraschino cherries
1/2 c. sugar
1/8 tsp. salt
1 tsp. vanilla flavoring
2 egg whites, stiffly beaten

"Combine sugar and water. Boil to soft ball stage (238° F.). Pour slowly, beating constantly, over egg whites. Add salt and fruits. Add fruit juice and flavoring. Mix thoroughly. Pour into tray of mechanical refrigerator or into freezer. Partially freeze. Carefully fold in stiffly whipped cream. Continue freezing until firm. 8 servings." [64]

Lemon Fig Ice Cream

1 c. whipping cream
1 c. milk
1 egg, well beaten
Few grains salt
3/4 c. sugar
1 c. chopped preserved figs, and juice
Juice 2 lemons

"Combine eggs, sugar, salt, figs and juice, lemon juice, and milk. Pour into freezer. Partially freeze. Carefully fold in whipped cream. Continue freezing until firm. 8 servings." [65]

Lemon Ice

2 c. water
1 c. sugar [Less sugar might appeal more to modern tastes.]
Few grains salt
6 tbsp. lemon juice

"Combine water, sugar, and salt. Heat to boiling. Boil 5 minutes. Cool. Add lemon juice. Freeze. 4 servings." [66]

Aunt Dora's Pulled Mints

2 c. sugar
1/2 stick butter

1 c. water
1/8 tsp. oil of peppermint

"If color is used, add at the first and cook coloring in. Combine ingredients. Put on stove and boil to 264° F. (hard ball). Pour out on marble. Cool 2 or 3 minutes. Make a fingerprint in the center of the candy and put in it 1/8 tsp. of peppermint. Fold all edges over. Pull until stiff, with little ridges. Stretch out on the edges of marble, away from the hot-spot. Cut with scissors. Leave on marble and cover with wax paper for the night. Store in airtight box. Might need to put a little butter on hands for pulling." [67]

Victoria Fudge

3 c. sugar
3/4 c. sweet cream
1 c. coconut
1/4 c. chopped candied cherries
1/4 c. butter
1/4 c. chopped candied pineapple
1 tsp. almond or rose flavoring
1/4 c. chopped figs

"Combine cream, butter, and sugar. Boil to soft ball stage (234 - 238° F.). Remove from fire. Cool to room temperature. Beat until creamy. Add chopped fruit and coconut. Add flavoring. Pour into well-buttered, shallow pan. Cut in squares." [68]

Lady Aimes Toffee

1/2 c. sugar
1/4 c. brown sugar
3/8 c. corn syrup
1/2 c. chopped raisins
Few grains salt
3/8 c. evaporated milk
2 tbsp. butter or butter substitute
1 tsp. any flavoring

1/2 c. chopped nuts
1/2 c. coconut

"Combine sugar, syrup, milk, and salt. Boil to hard ball stage (265 - 270° F.). Add butter or butter substitute, flavoring, chopped nuts, raisins, and coconut. Pour into well-buttered pan. When cold cut into long narrow bars." [69]

Uncooked French Creams

"Break the whites of three eggs into a bowl; add exactly as much water as you have whites of eggs (measure with the egg shells). Stir in confectioner's sugar until stiff enough to mold into any shape desired. Flavor to suit your taste." [70]

Cream Caramels

"Take one pint of cream and three pounds of sugar; boil together; add any desired flavoring; boil until it reaches 260° F. Pour out the mixture on flat dishes to cool, and, as soon as it begins to 'set,' which is very soon, cut it into little blocks with a sharp blade dipped in cold water. These will be good for some time, and are as healthy a confection as can be found for children." [71]

Tutti-Frutti Candy

"Chop seeded raisins, citron, figs and a few candied cherries. Put two cupfuls of granulated sugar and half a cupful of boiling water into a brass or porcelain kettle; boil hard for ten minutes. Take from the stove, pour into a bowl, flavor and stir rapidly with a spoon until it looks like cream. Add the chopped fruit and stir awhile longer. Press thin on buttered tins, cut into squares and wrap in waxed papers." [72]

Sea Foam

2 c. sugar
1/2 c. water

1 tsp. vanilla flavoring
2 egg whites
1/8 tsp. salt
1/8 tsp. cream of tartar

"Combine sugar, water, salt, and cream of tartar. Cover and boil 5 minutes. Uncover. Wipe sides of saucepan with a damp cloth. Boil without stirring to firm ball stage (245 - 248° F.). Pour slowly, beating constantly, over stiffly beaten egg whites. Add flavoring. Continue beating until candy holds its shape when dropped from a spoon. Drop by teaspoonfuls onto waxed paper. Sprinkle with rose-colored coconut."[73]

Divinity

2 c. sugar
1/2 c. corn syrup
2 egg whites
1 c. chopped nuts
1/2 c. water
1/8 tsp. salt
1/2 tsp. vanilla flavoring
1/8 tsp. cream of tartar

"Combine sugar, syrup, water, salt, and cream of tartar. Cover and boil 5 minutes. Uncover. Wipe sides of pan with damp cloth. Boil without stirring to firm ball stage (245 - 248° F.). Remove from fire. Pour slowly, beating constantly, over stiffly beaten egg whites. Continue beating until mixture holds its shape when dropped from spoon. Add flavoring and nuts. Drop by teaspoonfuls onto waxed paper, or pour into well-buttered pan. When cold cut in squares."[74]

Cherry Walnut Divinity

3 c. light brown sugar
1 c. corn syrup
1/8 tsp. salt
1 c. water

2 egg whites
1 c. chopped candied cherries
1 tsp. vanilla flavoring
1 c. chopped walnuts

"Boil sugar, syrup, salt, and water to firm ball stage
(248° F.). Pour slowly, beating constantly, over stiffly beaten
egg whites. Beat until candy begins to stiffen. Add candied
cherries, flavoring, and nuts. Drop by teaspoonfuls onto
waxed paper, or pour into well-buttered pans. When cold cut
in squares." [75]

Penuche

2 c. brown sugar
1/2 c. cream
2 tbsp. butter
1/3 c. coconut
1/3 c. chopped dates
1/3 c. chopped nuts

"Combine sugar, cream, and butter. Boil to soft ball
stage (234 - 238° F.). Remove from fire. Cool to room
temperature. Beat until creamy. Add fruit, coconut, and
nuts. Continue beating until mixture will hold its shape.
Pour into well-buttered, shallow pan. Cut in squares." [76]

According to legend the discovery of tea as a drink
occurred in 2737 B. C. when Emperor Shan-Nung was
boiling drinking water to purify it. Wind blew a tea plant
branch into the water, creating a splendid drink.[77] At first the
Chinese thought of tea as a stimulant and medicine, but
gradually they came to view it as a pleasant beverage.[78]

Tea was, however, unknown in Europe until 16th
century Venetians learned of it in China, and began to use it
for medicinal purposes. The Dutch can be credited with
actually introducing tea as a beverage to Europe. They began

importing it in 1606. Along with the tea leaves the Dutch merchants offered for sale Chinese tea ware in which to prepare and serve the exciting new drink. By the late 1600's tea was rapidly gaining popularity in England.[79]

The early Chinese tea pots were small red stoneware teapots. The cups were handleless. European silversmiths modeled silver teapots after the imports, and around 1680 the Dutch began selling their blue and white tin-glaze earthenware (ceramic) Delft teapots.[80] European manufacturers also produced hard-paste porcelain in the 16th and 17th centuries, two major makers being Meissen in Dresden, Germany and Sèvres in France.[81] The shape and decoration of the pots changed over the years — a globular shape becoming most typical. Individual Oriental-style tea bowls ("cans") evolved into cups with handles around the turn of the nineteenth century.[82]

In the 1760's Josiah Wedgwood developed a process enabling his pottery to mass-produce tea wares. His cameo reliefs on stoneware are now part of art culture.

In 1800 Josiah Spode began the production of porcelain containing bone ash. Such "bone" china is most delicate, almost translucent, and very collectible.[83]

As elegant "at homes" became the rage, more and more tea (and coffee) paraphernalia was produced. In addition to earthenware, Delft, and majolica, teapots of silver, pewter, and brass were marketed. Pottery and porcelain names sound like a litany to the souls of tea ware *cognoscenti* — Staffordshire or Canton blue and white beauties, a gleaming example of Tea Leaf lusterware, a French Haviland porcelain, a piece of English Minton, an Irish Bellock tea service . . . . A museum in the City Hall in Trenton, Tennessee, now displays 525 rare *veilleuse-théières* or "night light" porcelain teapots. These dual-purpose vessels were used to brew and serve herbal and floral teas, and to keep medication warm for babies. The tall base or stand of these teapots contained a *godet* or cup in which was oil, wick, or a candle. The flame in the base provided heat, and illumination — hence the name "night light" teapot.[84]

Lovely tea ware gave just the right touch to the hospitable custom of teatime. In the 19th-century novel *Portrait of a Lady*, Henry James wrote, "There are few hours more agreeable in life than the hour dedicated to the ceremony known as afternoon tea." [85]

Hot Chocolate for Nursery Tea

4 squares chocolate
2/3 c. sugar
1/8 tsp. salt
3 c. water
8 c. milk
1 tsp. vanilla

Mix chocolate, sugar, salt, and water. Cook slowly and stir constantly until creamy sauce forms. Add milk. Cook until hot. Stir constantly. Add vanilla and serve. (Makes approximately 10 cups.)

Frances Parkinson Keyes is now remembered for her writing (***Dinner at Antoines***, etc.). At one time, though she was well known for her "At Homes" while a U. S. senator's wife. Mrs. Keyes attributed her reputation for "the best tea in Washington" to the method of preparation:

"The tea was brewed with freshly boiled water, in an earthen teapot which had been thoroughly rinsed and heated with freshly boiled water; and, after a few minutes, the brew was transferred to another hot teapot — it could be, and generally was, silver this time — so that it would not become bitter or overstrong. It was renewed, according to this formula, at frequent intervals; and a second jug of freshly boiled water always stood close to the teapot, so that those who liked their tea weak would not have to drink it full strength. The secret of my wonderful tea lay in nothing more or less than this meticulous care;

*plenty of persons could afford a more expensive
brand than I could; but it was casually made,
allowed to stand indefinitely, and replenished from
time to time merely by the addition of water which
might be hot, but which was quite frequently tepid,
and which was all to seldom freshly boiled. "* [86]

Now, take a few minutes. Go set the kettle on to boil.
Get out your favorite cup and saucer (or an entire tea service,
if you plan to take tea in style) and assemble your supplies —
tea, perhaps sugar or honey, lemon, maybe even cream or
milk. (Black heroine Harriet Tubman took her tea with butter
in it![87]) Make yourself a pot o' tea, the perfect antidote for
stress, so they say, or just a pleasure pause if you are not
nerve-wracked. (Don't be overcome by guilt if you use a tea
bag, or herbal tea, or even decaf — the idea is to pamper
yourself a bit, not to get into self-condemnation!) Just enjoy
some *cha* (Cantonese slang for tea), and read the last entry in
this book. It is a sweet vignette describing one aspect of our
Victorian forebears' sometimes very different priorities and
lifestyle.

*"'Pink Teas,' just now so fashionable, are
rather novel if carried out to the letter, and an
expensive way of entertaining, too; yet, as the old
saying is, one might as well be dead as out of
fashion. So all those who wish to be fashionable
come and listen, and I will give you a few hints in
regard to getting up a 'Pink Tea.' As a matter of
course the table linen should be pink; the dishes
also of a delicate pink shade, which you may
borrow for the occasion. Arrange the white cakes
on high cake-stands, lined with fancy pink paper,
or pink napkins, and put the pink frosted cakes on
low cake-stands lined with fancy white paper or
napkins. The flowers for decoration must also be
of pink. Serve the creams and ices in novel designs
made of pink paper, such as baskets, boxes,
buckets, freezers, cups and saucers, shells,
wheelbarrows, vases, etc. I am not able to tell you*